Picture History of the 20th Century

of the

20th Century

1900-1919

Richard Tames

SEA-TO-SEA
Mankato Collingwood London

This edition first published in 2006 by
Sea-to-Sea Publications
1980 Lookout Drive
North Mankato
Minnesota 56003

Library of Congress Cataloging-in-Publication Data

Tames, Richard.
  1900-1919 / by Richard Tames.
        p. cm. — (Picture history of the 20th century)
  Originally published: New York : F. Watts, c1991.
  Includes index.
  Summary: A look at the events that helped shape modern history as seen in photographs
  from the first two decades of the 20th century.
  ISBN 1-932889-69-8
  1. History, Modern—20th century—Pictorial works—Juvenile literature. 2. Nineteen
hundreds (Decade)—Pictorial works—Juvenile literature. 3. Nineteen tens—Pictorial
works—Juvenile literature. [1. Nineteen hundreds (Decade) 2. Nineteen tens.] I. Title. II.
Series.

D422.T26 2005
909.82′1′0222—dc22

2004064979

9 8 7 6 5 4 3 2

Published by arrangement with the Watts Publishing Group Ltd, London

Contents

FLIGHT SUB-LIEUT. R.A.J. WARNEFORD. V.C.

Introduction

Few English-speaking people who saw the dawn of the new century doubted that it would be one of peace, progress and prosperity. Looking back, it was clear that the years leading up to 1914 continued more or less the trends of previous decades. Then came "The Great War for Civilization," which cut history in half, disrupting millions of ordinary lives, crushing major empires and redrawing the map of the world.

At the British Foreign Office, when war was declared in 1914, Sir Edward Grey observed enigmatically "The lamps are going out all over Europe; we shall not see them lit again in our lifetime." The masses, on both sides, believed the war would be swift and cheap. They were to be swiftly but not cheaply disillusioned.

The drama of war obscured other changes, particularly in technology. In 1900, automobiles were still seen as expensive toys for the rich. By 1919, they were being mass-produced to revolutionize public and private transportation.

In 1900, only dreamers took seriously the possibility of manned flight in heavier-than-air machines. In 1903, the Wright brothers proved it was not a dream. World War I made air forces a strategic weapon in their own right.

In 1919, with the victory of Allied forces, statesmen assembled in Paris to construct a new world order out of the wreckage of the old. Inspired by President Woodrow Wilson's "Fourteen Points," they created a League of Nations to settle international disputes peacefully and to encourage international cooperation. Thus, the "war to end all wars" ended on an optimistic note even though the United States refused to follow Wilson's lead and join the League.

United States in 1900-1919

Under President William McKinley, the United States had gained an empire. To protect the Philippines, Guam, Hawaii, and Puerto Rico, President Theodore Roosevelt decided to build the Panama Canal, linking the Pacific Ocean and the Caribbean Sea and sent the Great White Fleet around the world as a demonstration of American naval power. With the admission of Oklahoma (1907), Arizona (1912), New Mexico (1912), and the purchase of the Virgin Islands (1917), the United States continued to expand.

Revelations of corruption in American politics and industry ushered in the Progressive era with much needed reform legislation. Presidents Roosevelt, William Howard Taft, and Woodrow Wilson supervised efforts to break up monopolies, conserve natural resources, provide protection against impure food and medicines, regulate interstate commerce, and establish a new banking system.

The United States did not take part in World War I until 1917, when mounting public sympathy for the allies and the resumption of German submarine attacks against American shipping put an end to the policy of neutrality. America's involvement proved decisive in winning the conflict and shaping the peace.

△Reluctant warrior, Woodrow Wilson's vision of a better world made him a hero to the war-weary peoples of Europe.

(Below left) Mexico's long revolution after 1910 created instability along America's southern border and led to armed U.S. intervention in 1914 (below) and 1916. Similar use of U.S. forces was made in Cuba, Nicaragua, Haiti and the Dominican Republic.

◁"Rough Rider" Theodore Roosevelt won the Nobel Peace Prize for negotiating an end to the Russo-Japanese war.

▽The flow of European immigrants into America reached its peak during these years.

◁The 50-mile Panama Canal was opened in 1914.

▽Booker T. Washington, pioneer of education for African Americans.

Germany – Empire to Republic

As continental Europe's most populated and economically advanced country, Germany was bound to have a profound influence on its neighbors. German supremacy in music, philosophy and science was widely acknowledged, and its pioneering programs of social insurance were much applauded. Its brilliant achievements in technology, design and the arts were, however, overshadowed by the anxiety created by the expansion of its navy and the high profile of the military in the conduct of its national affairs.

German involvement in the politics of the Balkans and the Middle East caused further alarm. War, when it came, was scarcely unexpected. Germany was well prepared, both militarily and industrially but, failing to achieve the swift victory that had been planned, was eventually ground down by the superior resources of the Allies. The result was the utter discredit of the Kaiser's regime and the emergence, in disaster and defeat, of a democracy which never recovered from the dismal circumstances of its birth.

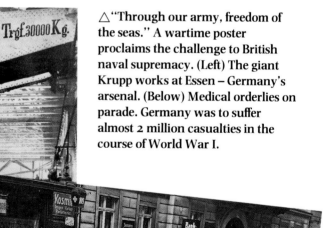

△"Through our army, freedom of the seas." A wartime poster proclaims the challenge to British naval supremacy. (Left) The giant Krupp works at Essen – Germany's arsenal. (Below) Medical orderlies on parade. Germany was to suffer almost 2 million casualties in the course of World War I.

▷ "The supreme warlord" – Kaiser Wilhelm II at the military maneuvers of 1910. Ambitious and impetuous, he refused to be restrained by the caution of his civilian advisers. After 1918, he fled to a long exile in neutral Holland.

▽ Political demonstrations in Berlin in 1919. The fall of the kaiser's regime created a political vacuum which favored the emergence of many left- and right-wing extremist groups. Violence on the streets was common and fed a widespread desire for a return to order and stability.

▷ A German warship awaiting demolition at Scapa Flow. Britain achieved at least one of its war aims in full – the destruction of the German High Seas Fleet, which had brought her to within six weeks of starvation through U-boat warfare.

Russia – from empire to revolution

In 1900, Russia was a vast multinational empire, less than half of which was Russian. Poles, Finns, Balts, Armenians, Jews and Muslims resented the official policies of "Russification," but found relative freedom in the inefficiency of the empire's sprawling bureaucracy. The disastrous Russo-Japanese war of 1904–5, and subsequent abortive revolution, forced the tsar into a halfhearted experiment of ruling the country through a parliament (Duma). Disaster for the Romanov dynasty might, however, have been avoided had Russia not become entangled in World War I. Operations were conducted with staggering incompetence, provoking a liberal-led revolution which ousted the tsar in order to fight the war more vigorously. Russia was, however, too weak to fight on and, in the chaos of disaster, a tiny minority of Bolshevik revolutionaries seized power and changed history.

△A rare photograph of the controversial "holy man," Grigori Efimovich Rasputin. He bewitched the Russian aristocracy and exerted immense influence over the tsar through his ability to control the effects of the tsarevich's hemophilia.

△The first Russian Duma (parliament) in session in 1906. Russia had no tradition of government by consent, and no effective method of cooperation between tsar and Duma emerged.

▷Doomed – Tsar Nicholas II and his family. The Tsarina urged him not to give concessions to reformers who wanted to ward off a revolution. The whole family was killed on Lenin's orders in 1918.

△At the Finland Station! A romantic view of Lenin, as seen by communist artist Khvostenko, addressing soldiers and sailors on his arrival from exile in 1917. The Bolsheviks' ultimate success was based on their willingness to destroy all opposition. (Above right) One of the most spectacular events of the 1905 revolution was the mutiny of the battleship *Potemkin*, later immortalized in a film by the Soviet director Sergei Eisenstein. This picture shows Matsushenko, the alleged leader of the mutiny who is said to have killed 10 officers. Rather than surrender the ship, he wanted to blow it up!

▷Alexander Kerensky (left) became Minister of War in the 1917 Provisional Government. He was determined to maintain Russia's commitment to the fight but by the time he seized the levers of power, they were no longer connected to anything that worked. His brief career was followed by lifelong exile.

End of empire – Austria-Hungary

In 1900, the Habsburg emperor, Franz-Joseph, ruled over a vast, shaky empire which stretched from the heart of Europe to the fringe of the Balkans. Power and privilege were virtually monopolized at the time by two nations which enjoyed special status – Austria and Hungary.

Vienna was the imperial capital but Budapest almost rivaled it in splendor, if not in size. Economic progress within the empire was very uneven, with islands of modern industry amid an ocean of peasant agriculture.

Cultural life, however, flourished. In Vienna, Sigmund Freud laid the foundations of psychoanalysis, while Lehar wrote lighthearted operas and Strauss composed dazzling waltzes. But even in the arts, new strains appeared as composers Smetana and Dvorak pioneered a fiercely nationalistic style of music among the Czechs.

The First World War broke the empire and its peoples seized a new future, while Austria was reduced to a small German-speaking republic.

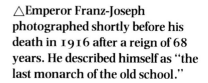

△Emperor Franz-Joseph photographed shortly before his death in 1916 after a reign of 68 years. He described himself as "the last monarch of the old school."

◁Early Polish postage stamps were hasty overprints of German stamps. This was symbolic of the chaos of the nation's rebirth. A modern stamp (top left) commemorates the hero turned dictator, Marshal Pilsudski.

▷Thomas Masaryk, the founder-president of Czechoslovakia, was born the son of a coachman. He rose to become a Professor of Philosophy and an outspoken champion for the Czechs. In 1908, he exposed official skulduggery intended to discredit Croat nationalists. In 1914, he fled to London to plead the Czech cause and in 1917 raised a Czech Legion among prisoners of war in Russia. In 1918, he persuaded the United States to recognize the independence of his nation and returned home as its president-elect.

◁Bela Kun (far right), with fellow communist revolutionaries in August 1919, shortly after his fall from power. While serving with the Austro-Hungarian army during World War I, Kun was captured by the Russians and returned to his native Hungary as a communist agitator, provoking the fall of a weak liberal government. Throughout the summer, the communists ruthlessly pushed through radical reforms and made many enemies. Invaded by Czech and Rumanian forces, and faced with a counter-revolutionary movement under Admiral Miklos Horthy, Kun's regime disintegrated when Rumania entered Budapest. Kun fled, via Vienna, to Russia.

End of empire – Ottomans

By 1900, the sprawling Ottoman empire had lasted for six centuries but was under pressure from within and outside. Britain had taken control of Egypt and Cyprus, and France had control of Morocco. Italy was to seize Libya in 1911 and the small states of the Balkans to struggle for the empire's last European territories in 1912–13. The response of the sultan's government was a policy of piecemeal modernization to make its armed forces stronger and its administration more efficient.

These limited changes encouraged a dissident group of young Turks to revolt in 1908, force the sultan to abdicate and restore the short-lived democratic constitution of 1876. The new regime's decision to ally itself with Germany brought short-term benefits but was a strategic disaster in the long run. World War I proved a great strain on the empire's shaky structure and provoked major internal upheavals, including horrendous massacres of the Armenian community. With Germany's defeat came humiliating peace terms and the dismemberment of the empire.

▽The Ottoman army was modernized to underpin the dynasty, but ironically its officers were to take the lead in limiting the power of the sultan. The army has continued to play a crucial role in Turkish politics ever since.

△Abd al-Hamid II accepted a democratic constitution on coming to power in 1876 but suspended it in 1878 and ruled as an absolute monarch until his deposition in 1909.

◁In 1915, the Allies tried to break the emerging deadlock on the western front by attacking the Gallipoli peninsula, with the aim of controlling the Dardanelles and thus a supply route to the Black Sea and Russia. "Johnny Turk" held the commanding heights bravely and the Allies, notably the newly-formed ANZAC troops from Australia and New Zealand, were pinned down on the beaches, where disease and combat took a terrible toll. The commander of the tough Turkish resistance was Mustafa Kemal, who was to lead the post-war revolt which created a new Turkish republic. He became its first president.

The Ottoman empire was dynastic and multinational. Its unity depended on the ability of its ruler to command loyalty or enforce obedience, rather than on any shared sense of national identity. Its ruling elite was mostly Turkish and Turks were a minority among the whole population. The British encouraged internal dissension among the tribes of the Arabian peninsula against their Ottoman overlords. The archaeologist T.E. Lawrence (right), a fluent Arabic speaker, proved himself a brilliant guerrilla leader, and became a legend among Arabs and British alike. Although his "desert revolt" was only a sideshow to General Allenby's methodical conquest of Palestine, it did arouse a wish for independent statehood among the Arab peoples.

End of empire – China

China's halfhearted attempts to modernize came too late to save it from imperialist predators. In 1895, China was dramatically defeated by a rejuvenated Japan and lost Taiwan to the victor. In 1900, a widespread antiforeign rising, led by a secret society of "Harmonious Fists" (hence the "Boxer" uprising), gained the support of the imperial court but petered out in bloody confusion. In 1911, a group of young Chinese, inspired by liberal political ideas of constitutional government, overthrew the Manchu dynasty. The provisional president of the infant Chinese republic, a western-educated doctor, Sun Yat-Sen, was obliged to give way to its leading general, Yuan Shih-kai. Yuan died in 1916, having failed to establish a new dynasty, but having set a pattern for warlord rule which was to curse the country for an entire generation.

Meanwhile, Japan had taken advantage of World War I to seize German-held territories in China and to press for "Twenty One Demands" which aimed to reduce the country to the status of a satellite. In 1919, Peking students protested against Japanese aggression and this "May the Fourth" movement broadened into a more general demand for change, which resulted in a Chinese communist party in 1921.

△Sun Yat-Sen in 1912. He spent 16 years in exile and led 10 abortive risings before attaining power – only to resign. Both nationalists and communists were to claim him as a spiritual father.

◁An official and his escort flee the ruins of Tsientsin. Note the telegraph wires – evidence of new western technology, alongside rickshaws pulled by men.

△Officers of the Manchu army
wearing western-style uniforms and
traditional pigtails.

△Demonstrators carrying
the new Chinese
nationalist flag.

△ Foreign troops arrive to
crush the Boxer Uprising

17

Birth of a nation – Ireland

The success of Irish Nationalists in forcing land reform in the 1880s encouraged them to press for "Home Rule." This provoked the creation of an Ulster Unionist party by Protestants determined to maintain the link with Britain. By 1914, both sides had built up private armies and civil war seemed imminent. The outbreak of World War I shelved the crisis and 200,000 Irishmen rushed to fight for Britain.

In April 1916, revolutionary Irish nationalists led by Patrick Pearse and James Connolly took advantage of British reverses in the war to launch an abortive "Easter Uprising" in Dublin. It was crushed in days, but the execution of its leaders created martyrs and a myth to rally mass support for total independence when the war ended. The 1918 election saw an overwhelming majority for Sinn Fein ("Ourselves Alone"), except in Ulster which remained solidly Unionist. The nationalists set up a Dail Eireann (Irish parliament) and prepared for guerrilla warfare.

△American-born Eamon De Valera addressing a Los Angeles meeting in 1919. He later became Eire's president.

▽This area of central Dublin was heavily shelled by a British gunboat during the Easter Rising in 1916.

△Sir Edward Carson, Unionist leader, addressing a Protestant rally in 1913. Their motto was "No Surrender."

▷ A pro-British account of the Easter Uprising stresses the sufferings of those caught in the crossfire. British troops were cheered as they put down the rebels, but the persecution which followed angered many. Although less than 1,000 people took part in the uprising, over 2,500 were arrested and 1,867 imprisoned. Although 90 were condemned to death, only 15 were actually shot.

THE SINN FEIN RISING AS IT AFFECTED PEOPLE

The number of rebels killed at Dublin is not yet known, but over 3000 were captured. The civilians murdered by them total 160, including twenty women. The casualties among the troops are 124 killed, 388 wounded, and 9 missing. Seventeen officers were killed and 46 wounded.

THE SHOT REBELS: THOMAS MACDONAGH (POET), "MAJOR" MACBRIDE, EDWARD DALY, T. J. CLARKE AND JOSEPH PLUNKETT (POET)

FIREWOOD GATHERERS

THE WIDOW'S LOAF

THE IMPROVISED POST-BAG · THE REAL SUFFERERS: HUNGRY CHILDREN RECEIVING A DOLE OF BREAD · THE CHILDREN'S BITE

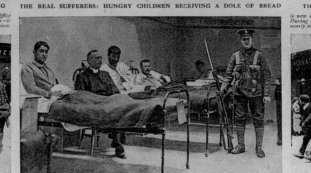
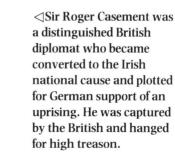

THE PRIEST AS PACIFIER · WOUNDED REBELS UNDER GUARD IN A TEMPORARY HOSPITAL AT THE CASTLE · REBELS UNDER GUARD

◁Sir Roger Casement was a distinguished British diplomat who became converted to the Irish national cause and plotted for German support of an uprising. He was captured by the British and hanged for high treason.

World War I

Sparked by a system of alliances and the rise of nationalism, World War I claimed the lives of at least 10 million men with twice as many injured. Everyone expected the conflict to be bloody but no one anticipated that it would last four long years or that soldiers, burrowed in trenches, would fight to gain yards, not miles, of territory.

The Central Powers – Germany, Austria-Hungary, and Turkey – fought the Allies – France, Britain, Russia, Italy, Japan, and the United States. Important campaigns took place in Europe and the Middle East while peripheral fighting ranged from Africa to China. Zeppelins, fighter planes, and long-range bombers added a new dimension to the conflict while the submarine altered naval warfare. Poison gas and tanks were two other World War I innovations. In 1917, Russia, in the midst of a revolution, withdrew from the conflict, but the Americans arrived in time to help foil a German offensive in the Spring of 1918. With a series of counter-attacks the Allies gained a decisive victory.

◁General John J. ("BlackJack") Pershing led the American Expeditionary Force.
▽A file of weary British "Tommies" slog through a wasted countryside.

△Police arrest the Serbian assassins of Archduke Franz Ferdinand (top), heir to the Austrian throne, who was shot when he and his wife visited recently annexed Sarajevo.

▷The British liner *Lusitania* was sunk in May 1915 by a German U-boat with the loss of 1,195 lives, 128 of whom were American citizens. The United States was outraged.

LEST WE FORGET

The Sinking of the Lusitania.
May 7th 1915.

▽Gas was first used by the Germans in April 1915, causing panic and many casualties among Allied troops. Primitive masks were rapidly developed. In the long run, however, the tank (below right), a British invention, proved more decisive in battle.

Votes for women

Nineteenth-century reformers established women's rights to education, property and entry to professions, such as medicine. By 1900, the struggle for further emancipation had come to focus on the suffrage. By 1914, women had full voting rights in 12 states, but many in the women's movement found this piecemeal change too slow.

The movement met fierce resistance and was divided over tactics. The "suffragists" believed that only strictly legal methods, such as petitions and public meetings, should be used. To do otherwise would be to discredit the cause and prove that women were too emotional to play a responsible part in public life. The "suffragettes," having tried constitutional means and found them futile, were willing to turn to direct action, though their attacks were on property, not people. During World War I, the campaigners supported the war effort to prove that women were worthy of citizenship. With passage of the 19th Amendment in 1920, they succeeded.

△In 1916, Jeanette Rankin became the first woman to be elected to the House of Representatives. She had led a successful campaign for women's suffrage in her home state of Montana in 1914.

◁Militant suffragette Alice Paul withdrew from the moderate National American Woman Suffrage Association in 1913 and helped to organize the more activist Union for Woman Suffrage. In 1917, she became a founding member of the National Woman's Party. In 1923, she managed to have the first equal rights amendment introduced in Congress.

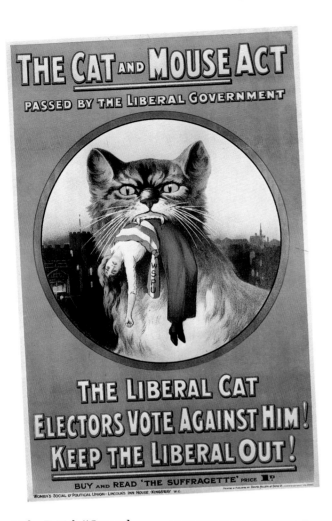

△American-born Lady Astor, in front of a painting showing her as the first woman MP to take her seat in the House of Commons, addresses an audience of university women at the University of London's Bedford College.

△The British "Cat and Mouse Act" allowed the release and rearrest of imprisoned suffragettes who went on hunger strikes.

▷ In 1917, four members of the Women's Party were arrested for picketing the White House, demanding voting rights. In prison they staged a hunger strike and were force fed.

The Automobile Revolution

At the turn of the century, there were only 800 cars registered in the United States and ten miles of paved roads. By 1916, there were 3.5 million automobiles on American roads. Taxicabs and buses were already transporting passengers.

The key to the automotive revolution was Henry Ford who produced the Model T, the first cheap, reliable car for the mass market. Initially priced at $850 in 1908, it cost only $360 in 1916. This was made possible because Ford devised the moving assembly-line which enabled his workers to produce a car in 90 minutes.

Other improvements also helped cars sales. For example, Charles F. Kettering perfected the electric self-starter that was to replace the cumbersome hand crank used to get the motor running.

World War I brought government contracts for trucks and ambulances which were later sold off as surplus. Many soldiers who learned to drive during the war used their new skills in civilian life as truckers, bus drivers, taxi drivers, and recreational motorists.

Motor vehicles had become vital to the American way of life.

△A showroom in London's fashionable West End advertizes an imported American car. Note the emphasis given to its proven reliability. A Rolls Royce cost over six times as much as this.

▷ British King George V being driven by C.S. Rolls in an early Panhard. (Below) The Rolls Royce Silver Ghost could travel at over 60 mph (96 kph). In 1907, the original model set a new reliability record of 14,371 miles (23,000 km) without a breakdown.

◁Family riding in a Model T Ford in 1914. "Any color you like as long as it's black" was the slogan. Over 15,000,000 cars were produced; many sold for as little as $360. The "Tin Lizzie" meant that owning a car was no longer the privilege of the rich.

△A 1912 Mercedes "Prince Henry Torpedo." The prestigious Mercedes marque (named after the manufacturer's daughter) was introduced by German motor pioneer Gottlieb Daimler.

△In 1917, there were 13,500 repair shops to service the 4.8 million motor vehicles registered in the United States.

▷In 1911, this photographic van took part in a parade to mark George V's coronation.

Humans Fly!

Manned, powered flight was first achieved by Orville and Wilbur Wright on the flat sands at Kitty Hawk, North Carolina, on December 17, 1903. The distance covered, 120 feet, was less than the length of a modern jumbo jet. A new age had begun but the world was slow to grasp the achievement of the inspired amateurs who had financed their pioneering experiments from the profits of a small-town bicycle shop. The first published account of manned flight appeared in a beekeeping journal!

Not until the Wright Brothers were managing flights of several miles and simple aerobatic maneuvers did the significance of their breakthrough gain acceptance. Military applications were thought to be of the most immediate value, and in 1908 the United States Army became the first armed service in the world to acquire an "air force."

In 1909, the Frenchman Louis Blériot flew across the English Channel in a plane of his own design. Rapid progress followed on both sides of the Atlantic. World War I accelerated this development even further, producing planes that were faster, larger, stronger and more reliable. The way was open for the birth of civil aviation as hostilities ended.

The TRANS-ATLANTIC AIR RACE 1919

Capt. J. ALCOCK, D.S.C.

ST. JOHN'S

LT. A. WHITTEN BROWN
CLIFDEN

LUNCHEON TO THE WINNER OF THE DAILY MAIL £10,000 PRIZE

Savoy Hotel, June 20, 19

▽Wilbur (standing) sees Orville pilot the *Flyer* into history. (Left) Wilbur at the controls dressed in ordinary day clothes. Specialized flying gear was developed later to keep out the intense cold.

△This autographed invitation shows Alcock and Brown's transatlantic route from Newfoundland to Ireland. Their Vickers Vimy bomber took 16 hours 27 minutes to complete the flight.

◁First flight of the Zeppelin airship at Lake Constance in 1900. This revolutionary ship, designed by former Germany Army Officer Count von Zeppelin, used lightweight aluminum and a gasoline engine. Commercial airship services using Zeppelins began in 1910. During World War I they were used to bomb Britain.

◁A fanciful view of Louis Blériot landing near Dover Castle after his 37 minute flight from Calais 23 miles away. In fact, his landing was anything but smooth and damaged his plane considerably.

△German air ace Baron von Richthofen (left), the "Red Baron," shot down 80 planes before being shot down himself by a Canadian pilot and Australian ground fire in 1918.

Science and medicine

To most people, the great advances in science and medicine made in the first two decades of the 20th century were quite literally invisible. This is because they involved the understanding or application of forces or substances which could not be detected with the naked eye. Radio seemed to be most immediately useful, although its applications were seen to be limited to controlling the movements of armies or of ships at sea. It was not until after World War I that it was thought of as a possible medium for entertainment.

The significance of the emerging discipline of nuclear physics, concerned with fathoming the structure of matter at the level of the atom and the universe, was far less readily grasped, even by the educated. In Germany, and to a lesser extent in America, politicians and opinion leaders had a growing respect for science. But in Britain, there was no attempt to draw up an official science policy until 1916.

◁ The sensational arrest of Dr. Crippen aboard a liner in 1910 – the first murderer to be caught in flight by means of radio. (Below) Guglielmo Marconi, the Italian inventor of "wireless telegraphy."

△ The three scientific papers published by Albert Einstein at the age of 26 revolutionized physics. In 1916, he published his *General Theory of Relativity* and went on to win the Nobel Prize for Physics in 1921.

▷ The career of (Lord) Ernest Rutherford illustrated the growing internationalization of science. Born in New Zealand, he is pictured here at McGill University in Canada. He went on to head the world famous Cavendish Laboratory in Cambridge. He won the 1908 Nobel Prize for Chemistry and developed the nuclear theory of atomic structure.

◁ Pierre and Marie Curie, discoverers of two new elements, radium and polonium, shared the Nobel Prize for Physics in 1903. After Pierre's death in 1906, Marie succeeded him as a professor of physics at the University of Paris. In 1911, she was awarded the Nobel Prize for Chemistry. During World War I, she set up an x-ray service, saving thousands of lives.

◁ Robert Koch, discoverer of the bacilli which cause cholera, anthrax and tuberculosis, won the 1905 Nobel Prize for Medicine.

△ Thomas Edison, the last of the self-taught inventors, seen here with the phonograph, one of his 1,300 patents.

Music and dance

Music in popular culture was changed forever by the development of recording and broadcasting. A patent on recording cylinders was granted in the United States in 1900. The 78 rpm phonograph record, which was to oust the cylinder, appeared the following year. By 1902, recording attracted the talents of world famous Italian tenor Enrico Caruso.

The first music radio broadcast took place in Austria in 1904, and in 1905 the jukebox made its first appearance in the United States. America set trends for musical taste throughout the affluent world. The full impact of these new marvels would not, however, be felt until the 1920s.

Most people still had to make their own music or rely on the skills of those who could. Many work groups and churches supported choirs or brass bands, and a piano was regarded as a highly desirable status symbol for the home.

There was, therefore, an immense demand for sheet music. In 1910, annual sales in the United States exceeded 200 million copies, and in 1918 the sentimental ballad *Till We Meet Again* sold 3½ million copies in a few months.

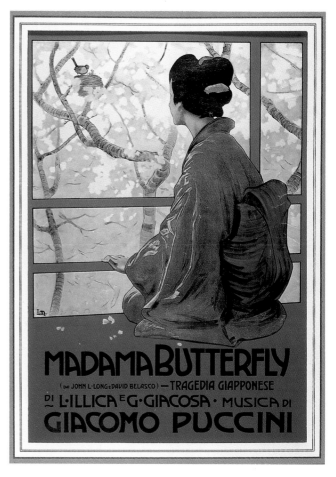

◁Recordings made Enrico Caruso known to millions who otherwise would never have heard him in one of his 50 opera roles.

△Puccini dominated opera with *Madama Butterfly* (1904). Russian dancer Anna Pavlova (below) formed her own ballet company.

△The unconventional dancing of Isadora Duncan shocked her native America but was applauded in Europe where she made a profound impact on dance education.

△The "Cakewalk" was one of many popular dance crazes to invade Europe from America. Like the "Turkey Trot" and "Grizzly Bear," it was intended to amuse the young, shock the old and be as different as possible from the formal elegance of the waltz.

▷Dancer/choreographer Vaslav Nijinsky was the star of the famed Ballets Russes established in Paris in 1909 by impresario Sergei Diaghilev, whose lavish productions revolutionized ballet and attracted such talents as stage designers Picasso and Matisse and composers Debussy and Ravel. Nijinsky created the role of Petrouchka, but his career ended in 1919 with the onset of madness.

NIJINSKI, dans l'"Après-Midi d'un Faune"
Aquarelle originale de Léon Bakst.

Sports

The opening decades of the twentieth century drew spectators to a wide range of new athletic competitions. Baseball's World Series began in 1903. The next year, the Olympic Games were finally held on American soil, with the nation's athletes winning 21 medals. The running of the Indianapolis 500 auto race (1911) and the first annual Tournament of Roses Association football game (1916) also attracted sports fans. The American League, the Professional Golfers Association, the National Collegiate Athletic Association were some of the sports organizations formed during these years.

The era produced its share of legendary sports figures. Denton T. "Cy" Young gained fame by pitching a perfect baseball game. In 1905, record-breaking Raymond "Ty" Cobb began a 24-year career in major league baseball. Barney Oldfield became the first auto driver to reach a speed of 133 miles per hour while Jim Thorpe triumphed in the 1912 Olympics. Knute Rockne was cheered as a football hero and went on to win acclaim as head football coach of Notre Dame. It was no wonder that Americans began to attend sporting events in record numbers.

△Jim Thorpe won gold medals for the pentathlon and decathlon at the 1912 Stockholm Olympics, but was stripped of them when it was learned that he had once played baseball semiprofessionally.

◁Sensation at the 1908 Olympics as exhausted Italian Dorando Pietri crosses the line first, but loses the medal because officials helped him. He was given a special gold cup in consolation.

▷May Sutton and Mrs. Hillyard (right) as doubles partners. Mrs. Hillyard was six times Wimbledon champion. In 1905, May Sutton became the first American to win the title and won again in 1907. Wimbledon became an international competition from 1901 onward. In 1907, every title "went abroad." A 1913 contest between New Zealander Tony Wilding and American Maurice McLoughlin drove Center Court ticket prices to an unheard of £10! In 1914, the Center Court was extended to take an extra 1,200 spectators. Wimbledon was, however, suspended from 1915 to 1918 because of World War I.

◁Jack Dempsey knocks out 35-year-old Jess Willard in 1919 to become heavyweight champion of the world. When he later retired, he became a successful New York restaurant owner. For many poor boys, boxing offered one of the few avenues to real wealth, but a career like Dempsey's was the exception, not the rule.

▷In 1919, major league baseball was rocked by scandal. Eight Chicago White Sox players, including leading hitters Shoeless Joe Jackson and Buck Weaver, were indicted for taking bribes from professional gamblers to throw the World Series. Although a jury acquitted them, baseball commissioner K.M. Landis permanently banned them from the game.

Hitting the headlines

By 1900, the newspaper was a 200-year-old invention – and just beginning to reach a mass readership. Compulsory education was creating something quite new in history – entire populations that were literate. The United States was one of the first countries to achieve mass literacy. As a democracy, it valued the education of its citizens.

American editors developed new attention-grabbing techniques, such as bold headlines, dramatic pictures and a terse, easy-to-read style. Other countries began to imitate these methods of boosting circulation. An American journalist of the period defined news as "whatever makes a reader say 'Gee whiz!'," so newspapers concentrated on reporting the real dramas of wars and natural disasters and the artificial dramas of sports and the social life of the rich and the famous.

World War I provided an ultimate source and standard of dramatic stories, eclipsing virtually every other news story. With the existence of nations at stake, the global conflict turned newspapers from an indulgence to a necessity, turning occasional readers into news addicts. Ironically, what should have been a force for enlightenment became a tool of propaganda as both sides controlled the press to sustain popular commitment to the war.

◁ The luxury liner represented the ultimate means of travel in terms of speed and comfort. The White Star liner *Titanic* was pronounced "unsinkable" at its launch. On its maiden voyage it struck an iceberg in the north Atlantic and sank within minutes. There were too few lifeboats to take its 2,224 passengers and over 1,500 people died.

▽In 1911, a fire broke out in the Triangle Shirtwaist factory, a New York City sweatshop, killing 146 employees, mostly young women. The tragedy made headlines nationwide and led to changes in local building codes and labor laws.

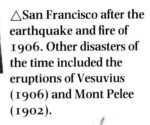

RUINS OF THE CITY AFTER EARTHQUAKE AND FIRE
SAN FRANCISCO, CAL.

△San Francisco after the earthquake and fire of 1906. Other disasters of the time included the eruptions of Vesuvius (1906) and Mont Pelee (1902).

▽Captain Robert Scott (center) with his expedition party at the South Pole in 1912. They found Roald Amundsen's Norwegian flag already there. All of the party died on the way home.

Birth of the movies

In the race to make "moving photography," Thomas Edison beat out the competition and produced the earliest films for the commercial market. His first feature was less than a minute long and showed one of his assistants sneezing. However, Edison's motion pictures had to be viewed through a peep-show machine. It was the French Lumiere brothers who developed projected films mass audiences could see at one seen by too many people at once to make any money. This left the way clear for the French Lumière brothers to develop projected films for mass audiences.

Another French pioneer, Georges Méliès, was the first to see the possibilities of trick-photography, which he used in his fantasy *Voyage to the Moon* (1902). Progress was rapid. gunman firing straight at the audience. American Winsor McCay's *Gertie the Dinosaur* (1909) was the first major animated cartoon offered to the public. It was made up of 10,000 individual drawings. By 1908, there were about 8,000 movie houses in the United States. They charged five cents a ticket. By 1912, daily attendance reached five million.

△Charlie Chaplin was the first motion picture "superstar." In 1913, he went to California and worked for the Keystone Company where he invented his famous baggy-trousered tramp character. He was a superb athlete and master of timing and gesture, much loved by World War I troops.

◁The spectacular set of D.W. Griffith's *Intolerance* (1916), a complex moralistic epic set in different historical periods, involved massive expense and a huge cast of extras. After the revolutionary Lenin saw this film he declared that motion pictures would become "the foremost cultural weapon of the proletariat."

◁Theda Bara – prototype of a new film phenomenon, the star created by publicity. Her real name was Theodosia Goodman; her stage name was an anagram of "Arab Death." It was claimed that she was the daughter of a French artist and an Arabian princess, although this was inaccurate. She appeared in over 40 silent films including *Carmen* (1915) and *Cleopatra* (1917).

◁A typically crowded scene from D.W. Griffith's saga of the American Civil War, *Birth of a Nation* (1914). Its sympathy for the Confederate point of view angered many but in doing so made movies an artform for serious discussion.

△David Wark (D.W.) Griffith raised the silent movie from the level of a fairground amusement to a serious form of art and the basis of a major branch of the entertainment industry. He was one of the earliest filmmakers to work in California and built up a brilliant team of players including Mary Pickford, Lillian Gish and Lionel Barrymore.

The arts

Developments in the arts were contrary. More people than ever before had the money, leisure and education to enjoy literature, music and art. Yet artists seemed less and less concerned in communicating with ordinary people. The advent of photography drove painters and sculptors to represent likeness through experimental techniques which could convey what they believed the camera could not – subtleties of light, mood and movement.

Literature perhaps stayed closer to popular taste than art or even the avant-garde music of a composer like Schonberg. But even popular writers seemed to comment on contemporary society in order to criticize its materialism and injustice.

Whereas the role of the artist had once been to celebrate the achievements of a people, it seemed that the painter or poet was someone who deliberately chose to live apart, uncomprehending of ordinary people and hard for them to understand.

△In 1907, Rudyard Kipling became the first English writer to win the Nobel Prize.

◁ *Troops Resting*, by C.R.W. Nevinson, Red Cross volunteer and war artist. Poet Wilfred Owen (below) was killed a week before the war ended.

▷ Picasso's "Harlequin."
Painted in 1918 – it
definitely doesn't look like
a photograph!

△Avant-garde Spanish
artist Pablo Picasso in
front of a poster for
Diaghilev's Russian ballet,
for which he designed
scenery and costumes.

◁American novelist
Upton Sinclair fought
social injustice in over 80
books.

▽Jack London rose from
poverty to become
America's most popular
writer.

Fashion

The invention of the sewing machine and the mass-production of military uniforms laid the foundations of the modern fashion industry in the mid-nineteenth century.

By 1900, a wide range of garments could be bought "off the rack," though it was still common for the customer to have a garment slightly altered to fit exactly.

In progressive circles, "dress reformers" promoted the view that clothes should follow the line of the human body rather than distort it with corsets, padding or elaborate decoration. The growing popularity of sports and belief in the value of exercise assisted the trend toward lighter, looser garments. The modern woman's suit, consisting of tailored jacket and skirt, evolved from formal riding clothes.

At the same time that women's outerwear became less fussy, glamorous crepe de chine lingerie began to replace the severely plain underwear of the past.

Men's clothing, by contrast, changed more slowly, although a "military" look was favored during wartime.

△Fashions for the year 1902. Note the S-shaped figure and pinched waist. Skirts reached right to the ground which made them impractical for outdoor wear. Note how high-necked the costumes are. Evening wear, by contrast, often revealed the shoulders. The wealthy wore different clothes according to the time of day.

◁Wealthy city-dwellers were dressing in much the same way throughout Europe and the Americas. In Asia, only the Japanese were beginning to dress like this family in Mexico City. Note that everyone wears a hat and that the ladies have long gloves. Lace was much used for decoration, although it was difficult to clean.

△Tennis was growing in popularity. The need for freedom of movement meant looser, lighter clothes. Note how this costume is trimmed in blue and white – a tribute to national pride in the navy.

▽Outdoor fashions for 1913. Note the contrasts with those of 1902 opposite – the whole line is softer and more flowing, shoes and necks are revealed. The hats, though still large, are less rigid and softened by feathers. Parasols were seen as an essential fashion accessory.

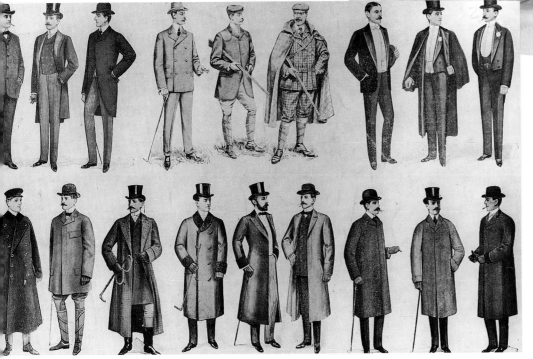

◁The *Tailor and Cutter* magazine of 1902 shows a full range of dress for the upper-class male. Only the model with the informal smoking jacket (third from right, top) does not have a hat – and even he is carrying one. Note the long, heavy coat and flat hat (first left, bottom row) designed for driving. Cars were open to the wind and rain and therefore very cold!

Growing up

One of the best things about growing up at the beginning of the 20th century was that children were increasingly likely to do so! Infant mortality rates fell rapidly as a result of improved diets and hygiene, better medical care and clean water supplies, even in the poorest slums.

Educational opportunities increased as states enacted compulsory school attendance laws. While children still labored in factories, they were now required to at least receive a grade-school education. John Dewey's theory of progressive education would reform the way children were taught by placing less emphasis on role learning.

Youngsters were treated to new toys, such as the Teddy bear and Meccano sets. They could join the Boy Scouts or the Campfire Girls. Children's literature flourished with the publication of L. Frank Baum's *The Wonderful Wizard of Oz* (1900), Beatrix Potter's *Peter Rabbit* (1902), Kenneth Grahame's *The Wind in the Willows* (1908), and Booth Tarkington's *Penrod* (1914). The first comic strip appeared in 1907. The new century brought new ways to have fun.

△J.M. Barrie's *Peter Pan*, or, *The Boy Who Wouldn't Grow Up* was an immediate success. A statue of Peter Pan was erected in Kensington Gardens opposite Barrie's house – overnight, as if by magic! Barrie bequeathed the valuable royalties from the play to the Great Ormond Street Hospital for Sick Children.

△*Meccano*, a constructional toy, was an indirect tribute to Anglo-American triumphs in engineering.

△ In 1910, William D. Boyce established the Boy Scouts of America, modeled on the British boy scout movement, founded in 1908 by Sir Robert Baden-Powell. The Campfire Girls was also chartered in 1910, anticipating the British Girl Guides by two years. The scouting movement provided a healthy and patriotic outlet for energetic youth.

▷ The price of a six-ounce bottle of Coca-Cola remained 5¢ for decades.

43

Personalities 1900-1919

Balfour, Arthur James (1848–1930), Conservative Prime Minister of Britain 1902–6. His diplomatic skill later made him Foreign Secretary (1916–19) and a leading figure at the Paris Peace Conference, as well as chief British representative at the League of Nations. He regarded the "Balfour Declaration" (1917) as his most important achievement.

Bethmann-Hollweg, Theobald von (1856–1921), German Chancellor 1909–17. Lacking experience in foreign affairs, Bethmann was pressured into war by the armed services, which finally forced him out of office over his opposition to unlimited U-boat warfare. As he had feared, that policy brought America into the war.

Clemenceau, Georges (1841–1929), Premier of France 1906–09 and 1917–20.

D'Annunzio, Gabriele (1863–1938), Italian writer and adventurer. Author of sensational novels, pioneering aviator and war hero, D'Annunzio led the seizure of the disputed city of Fiume (1919) before retiring into private life. He was chiefly responsible for reviving the Roman open-arm salute adopted by Fascists and Nazis.

Diaz, Porfirio (1830–1915), Mexican general and dictator. A radical turned reactionary, Diaz ran an efficient administration (1876–1910) which benefited foreign investors and oppressed the peasant majority.

Duncan, Isadora (1879–1927), flamboyant American who influenced the development of modern dance. She performed barefoot, inspired by classical Greek art.

Edison, Thomas Alva (1847–1931), American genius whose inventions included the carbon microphone, the record player, motion pictures and the perforated 35 mm film. He contributed to the development of the modern industrial research laboratory.

Einstein, Albert (1879–1955), German-American physicist recognized as one of the world's greatest scientists. His work on special and general relativity brought him international reknown. He won the Nobel Prize in 1921 for his work on the photoelectric effect.

Ferdinand I (1861–1948), King of Bulgaria from 1887 to 1918. The "Fox of the Balkans" made Bulgaria totally independent of the Ottoman empire in 1908, but chose the wrong side in the general Balkan assault on the Ottomans in 1912 and World War I. When his troops mutinied, he abdicated in favor of his son, Boris, in 1918.

Ford, Henry (1863–1947), American industrialist who perfected the assembly-line technique to produce the world's first cheap, mass-produced car. As an employer he was both enlightened and authoritarian, paying good wages and fighting unions.

Kerensky, Alexander (1881–1970), Russian politician who was catapulted to supreme authority in the chaos of 1917. His vigorous efforts to stay in the war led to an abrupt fall from power and exile for the rest of his life.

Luxemburg, Rosa (1871–1919), German revolutionary socialist. Polish-born and Swiss-educated, Rosa Luxemburg worked tirelessly to unite revolutionary socialists across national boundaries. Her militant opposition to war led to her imprisonment by the German government and her involvement in an abortive revolution led to death at the hands of right-wing Freikorps.

McKinley, William (1843–1901), President of the United States from 1897–1901. During his administration, the nation gained an empire in the Pacific. He was assassinated by an anarchist while visiting the Pan-American Exposition in Buffalo.

Pilsudski, Jozef (1867–1935), Polish statesman. A socialist agitator and

Isadora Duncan

Henry Ford

Theodore Roosevelt

nationalist revolutionary, he raised and led a Polish legion during World War I and was made head of state of newly-independent Poland in 1918.

Roosevelt, Theodore (1858–1919), President of the United States from 1901 to 1909. A dynamic character, "Teddy" Roosevelt was a cowboy turned soldier who became a crusading politician and died an explorer. An informed internationalist, he was the first head of state to win the Nobel Peace Prize in 1906, and was an early pioneer of environmental conservation.

Scott, Captain Robert Falcon (1868–1912), British explorer. A career naval officer, he led three major expeditions to the Antarctic, dying on his return from the South Pole.

Sennett, Mack (1884–1960), American film producer and director whose Keystone Studios made many slapstick comedies and launched the careers of Charlie Chaplin and Buster Keaton.

Smuts, Jan Christiaan (1870–1950), South African statesman. Having commanded Boer forces against the British, he worked actively for reconciliation after the war and led Union forces against the German African colonies in 1915–16. An influential member of the Imperial War Cabinet (1917–24) and Paris Peace Conference, he served as prime minister of South Africa between 1919 and 1924, before graduating to the status of a world statesman.

Sun Yat-sen (1866–1925), Chinese revolutionary leader and founder of the Kuomingtang (Nationalist) party. Elected Provisional President of China, he resigned for the sake of national unity.

Taft, William Howard (1857–1930), President of the United States from 1909 to 1913. A conservative politician, Taft vigorously supported antitrust policies but alienated progressive reformers. He went on to become Chief Justice of the Supreme Court.

Tarbell, Ida Minerva (1857–1944), a famous muckraker who exposed wrongdoing in industry. In 1904, she wrote the memorable *History of the Standard Oil Company*.

Taylor, F.W. (1856–1915), American industrial engineer. His innovative "time and motion" studies became the basis of a new approach to industry, summarized in his *Principles of Scientific Management* (1911), and used by manufacturers like Henry Ford.

Thorpe, James "Jim" (1888–1953), a great all-around American athlete. Winner of the 1912 Olympic Pentathlon and Decathlon, he was forced to give up his medals because he had played semiprofessional baseball. They were returned posthumously.

Togo, Heihachiro (1846–1934), Japanese admiral. British-trained commander of the Japanese navy that annihilated the Russian fleet at the battle of Tsushima in 1905.

Wharton, Edith (Newbold Jones) (1862–1932), American author noted for her novels about New York society. Among her best known works are *The House of Mirth* (1905) and *Ethan Frome* (1911).

Wilson, Thomas Woodrow (1856–1924), President of the United States from 1913 to 1921. A progressive and an idealist, Wilson supported measures to legalize unions, break up monopolies, and reform the nation's banking system. He led the United States into World War I but was bitterly disappointed when European leaders rejected his "Fourteen Points" for a just peace settlement and when the United States senate voted against American membership in the League of Nations he had sponsored.

Witte, Count Sergei Yulyevich (1849–1915), Russian statesman. A hard-working administrator who created the Trans-Siberian railroad, Witte was recalled to serve briefly as Russia's first Prime Minister.

Sun Yat Sen

Jan Christiaan Smuts

Woodrow Wilson

45

1900-1919 year by year

1900

- Antiforeign Boxer Uprising in China.
- Physicist Max Planck proposes the quantum theory.
- Paper clip patented.
- Olympic Games and World Exhibition held in Paris.
- Kodak Brownie Box camera introduced.
- William McKinley reelected as president of the United States.
- Assassination of Italian King Umberto I.
- Deaths of critic John Ruskin, composer Sir Arthur Sullivan and dramatist Oscar Wilde.

1901

- Commonwealth of Australia established.
- First escalator installed, in a U.S. department store.
- Safety razor invented.
- First Nobel Prizes awarded.
- First transatlantic radio transmission.
- U.S. troops crush nationalist revolt in the Philippines.
- U.S. President William McKinley assassinated; Theodore Roosevelt becomes president.
- Deaths of composer Giuseppe Verdi and artist Henri Toulouse-Lautrec.

1902

- Treaty of Vereeniging ends South African (Boer) war.
- Britain and Japan sign treaty of alliance.
- Beatrix Potter's *Peter Rabbit* is published.
- Animal crackers introduced.
- Deaths of diamond millionaire Cecil Rhodes and novelist Emile Zola.

1903

- Ford Motor Company founded.
- Jack London's *Call of the Wild* is published.
- The first World Series between American and National League teams.
- Wright Brothers fly first heavier-than-air plane.
- *The Great Train Robbery* opens at movie theaters.
- Williamsburgh Bridge opens in New York City.

1904

- Outbreak of Russo-Japanese war.
- First section of New York City subway system opens.
- Theodore Roosevelt reelected as president.
- Marie Curie discovers radium and polonium.
- Olympic Games held in St. Louis, Missouri.

1905

- Norway becomes independent of Sweden.
- Albert Einstein formulates *Special Theory of Relativity*.
- Deaths of writers Jules Verne and Lew Wallace.

1906

- First voice and music radio broadcast in the U.S.
- Earthquake devastates San Francisco.
- Russia's first elected parliament (Duma) opens.
- Deaths of dramatist Ibsen and painter Cezanne.

1907

- Oklahoma becomes the 46th state.
- First Ziegfield Follies opens.
- Gandhi leads civil disobedience campaign in South Africa.
- First celebration of Mother's Day.
- Deaths of composer Edvard Grieg and scientist Lord Kelvin.

1908

- Young Turks' revolt limits power of Ottoman Sultan Abdul Hamid II.
- Austria-Hungary annexes provinces of Bosnia and Herzegovina.
- William Howard Taft elected as U.S. president.
- Kenneth Grahame's *The Wind in the Willows* is published.
- Death of composer Rimsky-Korsakov.

1909

- Louis Blériot flies the English Channel.
- First animated cartoon shown in the U.S.
- Manhattan Bridge opens in New York.
- American Commander Robert E. Peary reaches the North Pole.
- National Association for the Advancement of Colored People established.

1910

- Union of South Africa established.
- Japan annexes Korea.
- Revolution overthrows Portuguese monarchy.
- Boy Scouts of America and Campfire Girls are founded.

- Radon discovered.
- Father's Day first celebrated.
- Deaths of Edward VII, nursing pioneer Florence Nightingale, writers Mark Twain, O. Henry and Tolstoy and painter William Holman Hunt.

1911

- "Agadir crisis" brings France and Germany to the brink of war.
- Manchu dynasty overthrown in China and a republic established.
- Triangle Shirtwaist fire leads to reforms in building codes and labor laws.
- First electric self-starter for automobiles.
- First air conditioner invented.
- Italy annexes Libya.
- Amundsen beats Scott to the South Pole.
- Assassination of Russian Premier Peter Stolypin.
- Deaths of composer Mahler and writer/librettist W.S. Gilbert.

1912

- U.S. Public Health Service is established.
- Arizona becomes the 48th state.
- Albania declares its independance.
- Woodrow Wilson elected as U.S. president.
- Sinking of the *Titanic*.
- First use of zippers in clothing.

1913

- Panama Canal completed.
- Ford Motor Company introduces moving assembly line.
- New York's Grand Central Station opens.
- Deaths of explorer Captain Robert Scott, financier J.P. Morgan, and inventor Rudolf Diesel.

1914

- Ireland on the brink of civil war.
- Outbreak of World War I.
- Anglo-French forces halt German advance at Battle of the Marne.
- U.S. Federal Trade Commission established.
- Panama Canal opens.

1915

- First use of poison gas in warfare.
- Liner *Lusitania* sunk by German U-boat.
- Japan's "Twenty-One Demands" – an attempt to reduce China to a protectorate.
- Deaths of poet Rupert Brooke and educator Booker T. Washington.

1916

- Battle of Jutland – major naval engagement of World War I.
- Battle of the Somme.
- First use of tanks in war.
- Abortive "Easter Uprising" in Dublin.
- Arab revolt against Ottoman rule.
- Albert Einstein proposes *General Theory of Relativity*.
- Woodrow Wilson reelected as U.S. president.
- Deaths of writers Henry James and Jack London.

1917

- The United States enters World War I.
- Revolution in Russia forces tsar's abdication.
- Italian armies collapse at Caporetto.
- Finland proclaims independence.
- Puerto Rico becomes a U.S. territory.

- George M. Cohan writes *Over There*.
- Deaths of showman "Buffalo Bill" Cody, painter Edgar Degas and sculptor Auguste Rodin.

1918

- Treaty of Brest-Litovsk ends war between Bolshevik Russia and Central Powers.
- Civil war in Russia leads to murder of tsar and his family.
- President Woodrow Wilson proposes Fourteen Points, a plan for world peace.
- Austria becomes a Republic.
- T.E. Lawrence leads Arabs into Damascus.
- Germany accepts terms of Allied armistice.
- Deaths of composer Claude Debussy, and poet Joyce Kilmer.

1919

- Communist rising crushed in Germany.
- Treaty of Versailles signed in Paris.
- Amritsar massacre – British forces kill unarmed Indian demonstrators.
- First airline links established between London and Paris.
- Alcock and Brown fly the Atlantic nonstop.
- Paris Peace Conference redraws European frontiers.
- Worldwide influenza epidemic.
- White Sox scandal.

Index